CHARLES DICKENS

To find in a day, a moment, a passing imag
very spring and source of his creativity; an
details, too, the figure of the movi

D1495945

ABOVE:

A coloured lithograph of Dickens. The words are from Dickens *by Peter Ackroyd.*

Michael St John Parker

Shortly after Charles Dickens was born, his family moved to Kent, where his father, John Dickens, a clerk in the Navy Pay Office, had been given a good post. They settled happily into 2 Ordnance Terrace, Chatham; across the road from the house was a big hayfield, covered in summer-time with buttercups and daisies, and in the distance was the winding River Medway, with the sailing-ships gliding up and down. The five years spent at Chatham were perhaps the happiest of Dickens' whole life. Visiting the dockyard – the Gun Wharf, the rope walk – with his father, cruising in the Admiralty yacht to Sheerness, wandering in the woods and parkland round the great house at Cobham, exploring the drowsy old cathedral city of Rochester, with its crumbling castle circled by cawing rooks, he spent the impressionable years from five to ten in what seemed during later life an idyllic dream.

He went to school in Chatham; but formal education was never very important to him. Something that mattered to him much more was the discovery in an attic of a heap of old novels, which he devoured passionately, living the characters for days at a time.

Hard facts soon came to provide quite enough stimulation for a child's mind. John Dickens was always a free-spending man, and

a bad manager, and the family's finances were in a poor state by the time that they moved to London in 1822. The modest comfort of Chatham was replaced by near-squalor in Camden Town, schooling was discontinued, and Charles became acquainted with a pawn shop, and did odd jobs about the house. Then, as the load of debt mounted, his parents found him a job with a firm manufacturing blacking at Hungerford Stairs, near the site of the present Charing Cross Station. The work was not specially hard – he had to seal and label pots of the blacking – but the conditions were sordid (he never forgot the smell of the sealing-cement and the noise of the rats which infested the rotten warehouse), the other boys and men employed at the place were a rough, coarse lot (one of the boys was called Bob Fagin), and to the dreamy, gentle child, still dazed by the ending of his Kentish idyll, the place became a complete hell of degradation and despair.

Meanwhile his father's troubles came to a climax with his imprisonment in the Marshalsea debtors' prison. The family was temporarily broken up, and Charles had to live alone in lodgings. After working during the day at Warren's blacking warehouse, he would visit his father in the prison, where the misery of the human wreckage he saw there made an indelible impression on his mind.

Although this incident loomed so large that it later seemed to Dickens to have

occupied ages of time, it was ended after about six months by John Dickens' release, which enabled him to discover his son's misery – for the first time! – and to take him away from the warehouse. In some ways, though, this led to the worst blow of all, for Mrs Dickens wanted the boy to go back to work, saying that they could not afford to lose the money. Charles could never forgive her this hardness. But his father for once put his foot down, and the boy was sent to a proper school.

Dickens stayed at Wellington House Academy from 1824 to 1827. The boy owed little to the place; but it compared well with Warren's, and he was happy enough – and it had at least the merit that it fitted him up for his first attempt at a regular career, which began at the age of fifteen when he was given a post in a solicitor's office. This experiment lasted nearly two years, but Dickens was temperamentally unsuited to such work, and developed a marked and enduring dislike of the law and lawyers.

In a manner typical of his age, though, he was resolved to better himself, and was prepared to labour furiously hard to acquire the necessary new skills. He mastered a system of shorthand so complex that it was said to be as hard as learning six foreign languages, and branched out as a freelance law reporter. In this he found much material for his later books; he was also confirmed in his contempt for the law and the legal system of the time – a contempt which was extended during the period 1830–3 to Parliament, when he became a Parliamentary reporter, working first for a journal called *The Mirror of Parliament* and then for the *Morning Chronicle* (1833–35), with whom he was so successful that he achieved something like the status of today's special correspondents. This period was of the greatest importance to Dickens' development as an author. His interests widened, he mastered the art of rapid, fluent, popular writing, and he acquired a stock of experience that gave his novels their tremendous 'immediacy' and impact.

By contrast to this positive experience, however, the years 1829–33 saw the gradual development of a situation which may almost vie with the episode of the blacking factory in

Dickens' first love was Maria Beadnell, who teased and tormented him for four years before finally rejecting him. Photographed here after her marriage to Henry Lewis Winter, she begins already to suggest the fat and foolish Flora Finching in Little Dorrit.

An imaginative depiction of Dickens as, 'with fear and trembling', he delivers his first manuscript.

the harm it did to Dickens' happiness. He fell in love with a girl named Maria Beadnell, a pretty, petite brunette with a lively and flirtatious manner. She seems to have teased or encouraged him largely for her own amusement, keeping him in suspense and finally dismissing him with casual thoughtlessness. The tragedy was that Dickens failed to get over it; his rejection crippled his capacity for affection, so that even the people who knew him best in after life would notice, and sometimes complain about, an inner reserve which prevented him from committing himself fully to anyone ever again. He made an ill-judged marriage on the rebound, and failed to find release either in that or in the affair which was the immediate cause of the breakup of his marriage. His children, to whom he was devoted, suffered from the same cause. And as a writer, he was to prove incapable of depicting satisfactorily an adult love affair. His deepest feelings hereafter are expressed in terms of brother–sister relationships.

Dickens' first attempt at writing fiction, as opposed to news reporting, was a short story published anonymously and without payment in 1833, in an obscure periodical called *The Monthly Magazine.* The editor requested more, and Dickens was only too glad to oblige, drawing on his experiences of London life in a manner that quickly caught attention for the freshness and wit of its observation. Early in 1834 he began to sign himself with the pen-name 'Boz' – a nickname borrowed from his younger brother Augustus.

At the beginning of 1835 he was invited to contribute regularly to a new daily paper, the *Evening Chronicle,* and in 1836 two series of *Collected Sketches By Boz* were published amid applause from critics and public alike.

The *Sketches* were collections of short essays describing contemporary London people and manners. They show Dickens graduating from reporting to authorship through journalism; but although he was to develop considerably beyond this point, the *Sketches* already bear the clear stamp of his unmistakable genius, with its sharp eye for a salient point and its direct, telling style. He had established himself as a budding author.

Writing commitments and contacts with publishers and editors now multiplied, and led during 1836–7 to problems of conflicting obligations, disputes over ownership of copyrights, and quarrels over payment, all complicated by the continuous rise of Dickens' reputation, which was at least matched by his equally rapidly rising opinion of what was due to him. With the help of a journalist who subsequently became his best friend and devoted biographer, John Forster, he fought his way out of difficulties, and emerged triumphant. In these few short months he turned into a fiercely aggressive, money-conscious businessman of an author, partly no doubt in reaction against his father's example, but also very much in tune with the self-helping spirit of the age.

He had another motive for financial toughness, however, in that he became engaged in the spring of 1835 to Catherine Hogarth, daughter of the editor of the *Evening Chronicle*. They were married on 2 April 1836, and spent a brief honeymoon near Chatham, before setting up house in Dickens' former bachelor chambers in Furnival's Inn, where they were joined by Catherine's 16-year-old sister Mary. This was a curious triangular connection; Dickens found little intellectual companionship in his wife – indeed he hardly seems to have asked for it; instead, he developed an intense platonic relationship with Mary, and was completely shattered by grief when she died with startling suddenness on 7 May 1837. The memory of Mary remained an influence on him throughout his life – it inspired him, for example, to write that supreme example of Victorian sentiment, Little Nell's deathbed scene in *The Old Curiosity Shop* – and years later he was still racked by the thought of his loss; on one occasion in Italy, he was convinced that he saw her ghost. But a third Hogarth sister, Georgina, gradually grew up to occupy a similar position in his affections and his household, and she was with him when he died.

Early in 1837 Dickens had established a home for his family at 48 Doughty Street, a comfortable town house, where he lived during the crucial two years when he was writing *Pickwick Papers*, *Oliver Twist* and

LEFT:
No 48 Doughty Street was Dickens' home from 1837–39. Here were played out the emotion-racked early years of his marriage. The house is now a museum boasting a magnificent collection of Dickensian relics.

ABOVE:
Catherine Hogarth, the eldest of three sisters, married Charles Dickens on 2 April 1836.

ABOVE:
Mary, second of the three Hogarth sisters, brought sparkle and vivacity to the novelist's home during 1836/7 'sympathising with all my faults and feelings more than anyone I knew ever did or will'. Her sudden death at the age of 18 shocked Charles Dickens profoundly.

Nicholas Nickleby, and thus rising to fame. There Mary Hogarth died, and the second and third of Dickens' children were born. There also Dickens entertained many of the artistic and literary celebrities of his time.

By 1837, Charles Dickens was writing with furious energy, so that the books came pouring off the presses. Many Victorians seem to have shared an amazing capacity for laborious work, but Dickens' vigour was almost frantic. When not writing, he would pace the streets of London, sometimes from dusk to dawn, working off the inner tumult of his mind, but also tirelessly collecting fresh material. Or he would ride twenty miles out into the country for lunch, and gallop back for supper, always observing as he went. This ceaseless activity of exploration, which we can trace back to his first days in London as a child of ten, made Dickens perhaps the most knowledgeable man of his time on the pulsating, swarming life of the capital city, its river, and the countryside around. He is above all the novelist of London, and for many people almost the genius of the place.

Meanwhile success – for *Sketches By Boz* was followed immediately by *Pickwick Papers* and worldwide celebrity – brought Dickens into social demand. Invitations poured in from the smart literary hostesses, and Dickens rubbed shoulders with the great – usually unaccompanied by Catherine, who was pregnant more often than not, and neither enjoyed smart society nor shone in it. However, although Dickens was sociable, he was no socialite; in fact he never had much to do with the aristocracies of wealth or blood.

Pickwick Papers came out in a series of monthly numbers between April 1836 and November 1837. This periodical method of publication had once been popular, but was thought obsolete when Dickens revived it for *Pickwick*. It became his regular style, enabling him to write and print continuously, often two books at a time. The continuing cycle of work stimulated him and acted as a healthy discipline; it also imposed a certain pattern on his books. The first of these serial efforts, Pickwick, was naturally rather experimental. It began with a publisher's proposal to write text for the illustrations of a well-known artist; Dickens rode roughshod over this idea, and insisted that the author must hold the initiative. (The poor artist subsequently shot himself.) The episodes were allowed to follow each other without much regulation, and there were numerous digressions and insertions.

Dickens used to refer to himself, among friends at least, as 'the Inimitable'. This was hardly modest; but nor was it exactly boastful. From the time of *Pickwick Papers*, Dickens was aware of his immense powers, and with outspoken Victorian confidence valued himself publicly at his own true worth. He knew that he was great.

And the Victorian public agreed with him. Not that they took him simply at his word – they read for themselves, and formed their own judgements, much more actively perhaps than their television-fuddled descendants of today. Their esteem was expressed in the eagerness with which they bought the novels as they appeared. After a shaky start, the sale of *Pickwick Papers* rapidly rose to 40,000 copies per issue.

Oliver Twist (monthly, February 1837 to March 1839) represented a deliberate change from the comedy of *Pickwick* to purposeful,

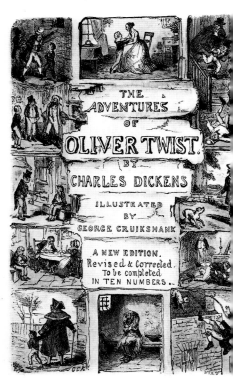

serious, realistic portrayal of social problems, and shows Dickens in one of his principal roles, that of an ardent social reformer. To the horror of the well-to-do, many of whom were amazingly ignorant of the realities that lay on their doorsteps, the book exposed some of the appalling misery that can lurk beneath the surface of a prosperous and apparently successful society. Poor Law workhouses, deserted children, prostitutes and criminals are the subjects of *Oliver Twist*. It was no accident that from 1839 onwards Dickens spent more and more of his time and money in practical philanthropy among orphans, prostitutes, and similar human derelicts, often in

collaboration with a remarkable woman named Angela Burdett Coutts.

A similar sense of crusading zeal can be seen in parts of *Nicholas Nickleby* (monthly, April 1838 to October 1839), where Dickens attacks the scandal of the private schools in Yorkshire which provided dumping grounds, and sometimes graves, for unwanted children. But there is in addition a fascinatingly revealing treatment of romantic love – its ecstasies and idiocies, and the darker side as well – and, as a subordinate theme, the theatre. From his childhood days in Chatham, Dickens was devoted to the theatre, both as spectator and as actor. In 1830 he was offered an audition at the Lyceum, and if he had not been prevented by bad health from taking it up, he might have embarked on a stage career. The best actors of his day were convinced, when they attended his dramatic readings later in life, that he would have swept all before him on the stage; but the Victorian theatre was in a poor state, and Dickens' genius must surely have achieved fuller expression in writing his own novels than in acting other men's plays. The influence of the theatre can none the less be detected in his books at every turn.

LEFT:
This tranquil-seeming mansion was a school which served as the original for Dotheboys Hall, depicted by Dickens in Nicholas Nickleby.

BELOW, LEFT:
Oliver Twist asks for more. Dickens' story, scathingly illustrated by Cruikshank, provides one of the classic tableaux of nineteenth-century fiction.

BELOW:
Mrs Squeers administers brimstone and treacle to the pupils of Dotheboys Hall – an illustration copy by Phiz to Nicholas Nickleby.

BELOW:
1 Devonshire Terrace,
York Gate, Regent's
Park, a comfortable
house in one of the
smarter districts of
London, where
Dickens lived from
1839–51.

All this time, the Dickens' household was growing and, no doubt, becoming more demanding – ultimately it numbered seven sons and two daughters.

By the end of 1839 a bigger house was necessary and the family moved to 1 Devonshire Terrace, York Gate, Regent's Park. Here Dickens set himself up in a thoroughly well-to-do style, with his own carriage and groom.

But if 1 Devonshire Terrace was a prosperous home, it was not an entirely happy one. Though regarded in his own time as *par excellence* the novelist of and for the family, Dickens was dissatisfied with his wife, and all too easily disappointed by his children. This was one of the saddest of many paradoxes in Dickens' life.

The trouble with his wife was rooted in their incompatibility. In the early days, Dickens had sought no more than sensual satisfaction from Catherine; but this phase soon passed, and there was nothing to follow. The experience with Maria Beadnell had damaged Dickens emotionally, but it had not destroyed the natural high charge of his temperament, which found neither release nor understanding inside marriage.

There was, perhaps, an element of compensation in the great surge of feeling which

suffused Dickens' next novel, *The Old Curiosity Shop*, which was published in weekly instead of monthly instalments (April 1840 to January 1841), as the rather accidental result of Dickens' commitment to a failing magazine called *Master Humphrey's Clock*. It is nowadays the least regarded of his works, being an extreme example of a Victorian taste for sentimentality which seems to modern eyes insipid at best, and revoltingly maudlin at worst. At the time, though, it was incredibly popular; floods of tears were shed over the death of Little Nell, and swarms of boats put out from New York to meet the packet carrying the latest instalment.

Barnaby Rudge, also published weekly (February 1840 to November 1841), is one of Dickens' two historical novels – the other being *A Tale Of Two Cities* (weekly, April to November 1859). Dickens was drawn to the past, and tried frequently to write about it – the *Master Humphrey's Clock* project had been thought up with this end in view. But he had little feeling for the realities of history, and always tended unconsciously to gravitate in his descriptions towards the period around 1820–5, when he himself had been first so happy and then so unhappy as a child. Writing under the shadow of Sir Walter Scott, his historical works rarely achieved full power, though, interestingly, they are often appreciated by people who find his 'mainline' books unattractive.

After tremendous exertions, and success to match, Dickens went in search of change to the United States in 1842. He unreasonably expected to find the land of the free a paradise on earth, and when it did not come up to scratch he was equally extreme in his disappointment. He made matters worse for himself by rebuking the Americans in a number of public speeches for their flagrant disregard of the courtesies of international copyright – there was as yet no law relating to the matter – by which he and other authors were being in effect defrauded of their rights. The sharp satire of American philistinism in *Martin Chuzzlewit* (monthly January 1843–July 1844), his next big book, soured his reputation in America for some time to come, though relations were triumphantly restored before the end of his life.

LEFT:
Of all Dickens' novels, perhaps The Old Curiosity Shop *has been subject to the most extreme fluctuations of critical opinion. Overwhelmingly successful at the time of its first appearance, it has since been rejected as unreal and sentimental. But the old Tudor house which provided Dickens with the story's setting is still to be found at 13–14 Portsmouth Street, WC2.*

LEFT:
Two of Dickens' sons, Charley and Wally, and his two daughters, Mamie and Katey, sketched by his friend, the artist Maclise. Dickens took this picture with him on his visit to America. The family's pet raven, Grip, who appears in fictional form in Barnaby Rudge, *perches on the back of the sofa.*

Dickens' Dream

Hanging above the fireplace in the study at 48 Doughty Street is the painting called 'Dickens' Dream', by R. W. Buss. The author is seen musing in his chair, before the desk at which he wrote many of his novels, and surrounded by the teeming creations of his imagination. The desk (seen in detail above) carries the china monkey without which Dickens was unable to settle down to writing. The painting is unfinished, so that only a few of the scenes are fully developed; but this, if anything, enhances the dreamlike effect of the whole. It is part of the secret of Dickens' success that he was able to make his characters

'live' so vividly that they carry complete conviction. Most of them were to some extent based on real-life people, but Dickens invested them with an independent vitality that was in no way dependent on their origins. They lived with him as he wrote, and he seems to have been almost possessed by them. So Buss's rather literal-minded painting may convey an important truth about Dickens, namely the quality of his inner life – 'a kind of imagination, fed by the unconscious, that we do not expect to discover in a novelist', as J. B. Priestley says. Above all, perhaps, the painting conveys the delight that runs through all his creation: 'he enjoyed everybody in his books.' (G. K. Chesterton).

BELOW:
*Bob Cratchit and the
crippled Tiny Tim
hurry happily through
the snow to their
Christmas dinner in*
A Christmas Carol.

BELOW, RIGHT:
*Mrs Gamp, the
hypocritical old mid-
wife, with her huge
coal-scuttle bonnet
and her umbrella, as
she appears in* Martin
Chuzzlewit.

*I*t was while he was at work on *Chuzzle-wit* that Dickens began the series of *Christmas Books* that was to become so closely associated with his name. *A Christmas Carol* (1843), *The Chimes* (1844), *The Cricket on the Hearth* (1845), *The Battle of Life* (1846), *The Haunted Man* (1848) – they became an institution, and helped to form the very image of the Victorian Christmas itself. They are perhaps best remembered for their mixture of sentiment and the super-natural, their blend of melodrama and jollity; but they are also infused with a strong moral purpose, and in them Dickens expresses, almost more passionately than anywhere else, his sense of social right and wrong.

In 1844–5 the family spent a year in Italy, ostensibly for purposes of 'economy'; Dickens continued to write, though words came more slowly away from the inspiration of London's teeming streets. Early in 1846 there was a brief and unhappy involvement with editor-ship of a new national paper, the *Daily News*; then once more abroad – this time to Lausanne and Paris. In part these travels, which continued intermittently throughout the 1850s, mostly in France, were the reward of success; but one cannot avoid the feeling that they were also in part an attempt by Dickens to escape from, or at any rate mini-mise, the private pressures that life in London was bringing.

A new phase in Dickens' career as a novelist opens with *Dombey and Son* (monthly, October 1846 to April 1848). This is the first of his novels to be fully planned as a whole in advance. From now onwards it became his practice to select a theme (in this case Pride), and then to build round it a plot-skeleton before settling down to write; the detail would be added as the episodes evolved. In other words, Dickens was moving from mere sharp-eyed observation of life, to the creation of a dramatic-poetic work of art – something both infinitely more difficult and infinitely more rewarding.

David Copperfield (monthly, May 1849 to November 1850) at once became the most popular of all his works, and has always occupied a special position on the list. It was something special for Dickens, too, because while he always used his own experience as the mine of his imagination, here he wrote in a style much more directly autobiographical than we find anywhere else. His childhood happiness and misery, his mistakes in love, his father (as Mr Micawber – his mother had appeared long before, as Mrs Nickleby), all were displayed in character-drawing of dazzling charm and brilliance.

There was a darker side, too. Years before, when his own father had been jailed for debt,

Paul and Florence Dombey

Charles had of course been too young to understand the complications of the law of debt, and the prison system, both at that time sunk in unreformed chaos; but he could not have avoided being affected by their results, if he had been ten times less sensitive and observant than he was.

RIGHT:

RIGHT:
'Let us be moral.
Let us contemplate
existence.'
Mr Pecksniff in
Martin Chuzzlewit
is one of Dickens'
great creations –
almost the definitive
fictional hypocrite.

BELOW:
This building off the
Strand served as the
office of Household
Words, *the journal*
which Dickens edited
from 1850–59. It was
supposed to be on the
site of an old tenement
where the artist
Hogarth had seen the
final tableau of 'The
Harlot's Progress'.

That earlier period of Dickens' life may in fact be seen as providing a classic instance of the traumatic experience which scars an individual for life. In little ways (for years he would cross the Strand above Charing Cross to avoid the smell of blacking) and in bigger matters, it was with him to the end. Throughout his books he harps on the horrors of child-exploitation; on the fate of orphans and abandoned children – on the misery which can be the undeserved product of social circumstances; and on the effects of improvidence and debt. He tried to hide his own experiences from the world, though when the strain of suppression grew too great, he tried to relieve it by writing a fragment of candid autobiography. But he could not reveal himself so far, and sought refuge in a fictionalised account, exorcising the past by causing it to be relived by David Copperfield. Even this was inadequate, though, as we can see from Copperfield's cry of distress: 'The deep

1853) centres round the great contemporary scandal of the Court of Chancery, with its ruinous delays; more broadly, it denounces the destruction of the innocent by the impersonal working of an unjust society. *Hard Times* (weekly, April to August 1854) lies off Dickens' usual track, in that it deals with the industrial north, where Dickens' attention had been caught by a great weavers' strike at Preston. Its theme, though, is similar – the grim machinery of the new industrial society, and its soul-destroying effects on masters and men alike.

remembrance of the sense I had of being utterly neglected and hopeless; of the shame I felt in my position; of the misery it was to my young heart to believe that, day by day, what I had learned and thought, and delighted in, and raised my fancy and my emulation up by, was passing away from me, never to be brought back any more; cannot be written.'

During the 1850s he spent a good many months in Paris, or at a villa near Boulogne; but this middle period of his career as an author is marked by a vigorous devotion to work of three types at home, apart of course from the constant round of writing. First, he became heavily involved in a very professional sort of amateur theatricals; then there was practical philanthropic work; and finally there was magazine editing – first *Household Words* (1850–9), and then *All The Year Round* (founded by Dickens in 1859, and which maintained a steady circulation of 100,000), became national family institutions.

The force of Dickens' philanthropic convictions emerged with dramatic strength in his next three novels, which together form a dark and powerful group shaken by a fierce anger for social reform. *Bleak House* (monthly from March 1852 to September

BELOW, LEFT:
Little Dorrit leaving the Marshalsea Debtors' Prison, after visiting her old father. Another of the classic images of Dickens' fiction, and one which refers with particular poignancy to the author's own childhood experiences.

FAR RIGHT:
Ellen Ternan, the young actress whose affair with Dickens was the occasion of the collapse of the author's marriage in 1858. She remains an enigmatic figure, whose real role in Dickens' life may never be fully understood.

BELOW:
An early water-colour of Dickens' study in Gad's Hill Place. The writing desk and chair are now in 48 Doughty Street, London.

*L*ittle Dorrit (monthly, December 1855 to June 1857) focuses especially on the law of debt – a monster which Dickens had known all too well in his younger days. Its plot is admittedly weak: but it has recently been increasingly admired for the brilliance with which a wide range of characters are brought together to create a social panorama.

All three of these books make increasing use of symbolism and imagery. In *Little Dorrit*, particularly, philosophical and religious themes occur prominently. Dickens was not a profound thinker – in fact his notably middlebrow attitudes contributed a lot to his popularity. But he was compelled to contemplate ultimate realities by the problems he dealt with in his books, and, still more, by his own accumulating personal distress.

In 1856 he purchased a property which meant far more to him than any other. In that far-distant period of irretrievable happiness at Chatham, he had walked with his father by Gad's Hill, near Rochester. There they had admired an elegant little Georgian house, built of rosy brick and set among trees, with a white-painted cupola on the roof. 'If you were to be very persevering, Charles,' said his father, 'and were to work hard, you might some day come to live in it.' That was the sort of day-dreaming that the elder Dickens' life was largely wrecked on; his son, made of sterner stuff, did just as his father could never have done, and bought the house.

It is ironical that just at this moment which should have been so happy, Dickens' family life finally disintegrated. This seemed at the time to be a sudden catastrophe, but was in fact the result of a long process of alienation and deterioration. The matter has been obscured by Dickens' own secrecy, and the tendency of later generations to gloss over the episode. But it is now sufficiently clear that in 1857 he fell madly in love with a young actress named Ellen Ternan, whom he met while working as actor-producer on a melodrama by Wilkie Collins named *The Frozen Deep*. The trouble blew up rather suddenly in 1858, when Dickens separated from his wife amid tremendous family recriminations. Most of the Hogarths sided with Catherine, except for Georgina, who stayed with Dickens and indeed played a rather equivocal role in the affair. By agreement, Dickens kept most of the children, and there was an attempt to preserve appearances in public; but this broke down, and a massive public scandal followed, which affected Dickens painfully, not least because he felt that as England's family novelist he had a duty to his many devoted readers. The scandal was focused chiefly on Dickens' relations with his wife and her sister, and was substantially inaccurate. Ellen Ternan was hardly noticed in the uproar, but it is not easy to say whether this made matters better or worse. He set her up in a little house in Peckham in 1867, but neither of them seems to have derived much happiness from the affair.

ABOVE:
Charles Dickens with his daughters Mamie and Katey in the garden at Gad's Hill. They sided with him after their mother had left the family home – Mamie without reservation, though Katey later described her father as '. . . not a good man, but he was not a fast man, but he was wonderful!'.

LEFT:
Charles Dickens takes his ease in the garden of Gad's Hill Place, the house of his childhood dreams which he bought in 1856.

The shadow of all this lay over the last period of Dickens' life, the 1860s. He settled in something like isolation to write at Gad's Hill Place, and tried to break with the past; in 1860 he actually made a great bonfire of all his old personal papers. If he was tempted to become a recluse, however, other factors overrode the temptation.

His natural dynamism, and his love of acting, were reinforced by the heavy financial strain of supporting in effect three separate households, and together they provided the motivation for a series of dramatic readings from his own works, which had actually begun in 1858 and continued with ever-increasing triumph until his death. These readings set the seal on his reputation as the supreme literary genius of the time; they brought in fabulous sums of money; but they also ruined his health.

Meanwhile, his work as a novelist continued to develop, and, in *Great Expectations* (weekly, December 1860 to August 1861), it achieved perhaps its finest flowering. In this book we again find a reforming theme – the penal code and its effects. But this is much more than a social tract, and shows Dickens simultaneously at his most inventive and his

most purposeful, mingling concepts with observation in masterly profusion, and running the entire range from tragedy to comedy. Among the most impressive features of this late masterpiece is its subtle yet powerful irony, used not merely as embellishment but

as structure – a far cry from the riotous cari-
cature of *Pickwick*, the bitterness of *Oliver
Twist*, or the satire of *Nicholas Nickleby*.

Our Mutual Friend appeared monthly
from May 1864 to November 1865, although
it was written under difficulties – Dickens'
health was failing, his mind was troubled, and
he was particularly unnerved by a narrow
escape from death when he and Ellen Ternan
were involved in an appalling railway catastrophe near Folkestone in June 1864. The
book lacks drive and unity, though it contains
some good sketches. Even its weakness, however, becomes a source of strength – Dickens'
growing mental and spiritual disillusion-
ment led him here to write a damningly effec-
tive portrait of the character-disintegration
caused by an acquisitive society.

ABOVE:

Of all the mysteries surrounding Dickens' relationship with women, perhaps the most elusive concerns the youngest of the three Hogarth sisters, Georgina. She lived with the author's family from 1842, and seems to have supplied much of the intelligence, feeling and sheer social sparkle that her sister, Charles' wife, so conspicuously lacked. Georgina stood by her brother-in-law when the marriage broke up and was with him when he died.

List of Works

BORN PORTSMOUTH 7 FEBRUARY 1812

1836	Collected Sketches by Boz (published in 2 series)
1836–37	Pickwick Papers
1837–39	Oliver Twist Nicholas Nickleby
1840–41	The Old Curiosity Shop Barnaby Rudge
1843–44	Martin Chuzzlewit
1843	A Christmas Carol
1844	The Chimes
1845	The Cricket on the Hearth
1846	The Battle of Life
1848	The Haunted Man
1846–48	Dombey & Son
1849–50	David Copperfield
1852–53	Bleak House
1854	Hard Times
1855–57	Little Dorrit
1859	A Tale of Two Cities
1860–61	Great Expectations
1864–65	Our Mutual Friend
1870	Edwin Drood (unfinished)

DIED GAD'S HILL 9 JUNE 1870

His frightening energy – by now almost suicidal-seeming – drove him to the end. He spent 8 June 1870 writing busily in his chalet summer-house at Gad's Hill Place; then, at dinner that night, he had a stroke, and died quite quickly the next day. On the last page that he wrote, in the unfinished *Edwin Drood*, he described a bright sunlit day in Rochester: 'Changes of glorious light from moving boughs, songs of birds, scents from gardens, woods, and fields . . . penetrate the Cathedral, subdue its earthy odour, and preach of the Resurrection and the Life. The cold stone tombs of centuries ago grow warm; and flecks of brightness dart into the sternest marble corners of the building, fluttering there like wings.' The wheel had come full circle, and he was home.

His books have continued to grow in popularity. With the lapse of copyright, and the multiplication of translations into every language under the sun, sales have passed computation. In the Soviet Union alone, sales between 1945 and 1957 passed seven and a half million. The reasons for this continuing success vary, for, like all great geniuses, Dickens is himself infinitely varied. An example of this is the change in the critical estimates of his earlier as against his later works. Until recently, the early books were the more prized, for their superb vitality and irresistible humour; now it is the later books, with their mastery of character, their powerful depiction of life as it is lived, that attract attention.

Dickens has stood the test of a hundred years; there is no doubt that he will stand the test of many more.